W9-BQD-157

Growing up Safe

Safety hallowe'en

Illustrated by Sue Wilkinson

SAFETY SERIES

PUBLISHER	Joseph R. DeVarennes
PUBLICATION DIRECTOR	Kenneth H. Pearson
ADVISORS	Roger Aubin Robert Furlonger
EDITORIAL MANAGER	Jocelyn Smyth
EDITORS	Ann Martin Robin Rivers Mayta Tannenbaum
PRODUCTION MANAGER	Ernest Homewood
PRODUCTION ASSISTANTS	Martine Gingras Catherine Gordon Kathy Kishimoto Peter Thomlison
PUBLICATION ADMINISTRATOR	Anna Good
SPECIAL CONSULTANT	***Barbara Jarvis***
ILLUSTRATION AND DESIGN	Sue Wilkinson

Canadian Cataloguing in Publication Data

Main entry under title:

Safety at Hallowe'en

(Growing up safe; 9)
ISBN 0-7172-2455-4

1. Halloween—Safety measures—Juvenile literature.
I. Wilkinson, Sue. II. Series

HQ770.7.S333 1988 j363.1'3 C88-094233-9

Printed and Bound in U.S.A.

Come join Alex and Sarah Skunkerton as they find out everything they need to know about Hallowe'en safety.

ONLY A GROWNUP SHOULD USE A SHARP KNIFE TO CARVE A JACK-O'-LANTERN.

Now I'll light the candle and put the jack-o'-lantern on the front porch.

DO NOT TOUCH A JACK-O'-LANTERN WHEN THE CANDLE INSIDE IS LIT.

I really like this mask.
Can I wear it, Mom?

WEAR MAKEUP INSTEAD OF A MASK SO YOU CAN SEE CLEARLY.

Come on, Mom! We can't go without you.

ALWAYS GO TRICK OR TREATING WITH A GROWNUP.

Let me check out
your costumes, first.
They look great and very safe.

WEAR A COSTUME THAT ALLOWS YOU TO WALK EASILY.

27
I like your shiny strips, Alex. Where did you get them?

WEARING A BRIGHT COSTUME AND REFLECTIVE STRIPS MAKES IT EASIER FOR YOU TO BE SEEN AT NIGHT.

TRICK OR TREAT AT HOUSES WHERE YOU KNOW THE PEOPLE WELL.

REMEMBER ALL THE TRAFFIC RULES WHEN YOU ARE TRICK OR TREATING.

Cindy's house looks like a good place for treats.
Wait until we cross at the corner.
211

DO NOT CROSS AND RECROSS THE ROAD.

That looks like fun, Alex.
Can I have a sparkler too?

BE CAREFUL WHEN HOLDING A LIT SPARKLER. IT COULD BURN YOU.

991
BLOCK
PARENT
© BPPCI, 1968 TM

IF YOU DO GET LOST TRY TO FIND A BLOCK PARENT HOUSE.
The Block Parent will help her.
Look! The ballerina's lost.

IF YOU GET COLD, TELL THE GROWNUP WITH YOU RIGHT AWAY.

DO NOT EAT TREATS UNTIL A GROWNUP HAS CHECKED THEM.

That's enough for tonight.
Go brush your teeth and put on your pyjamas.

DO NOT EAT TOO MANY TREATS AT ONCE.

That was fun, Mom. Can we go trick or treating again tomorrow?
Once a year is quite enough. Sleep well.